David

Miller

350

Massachusetts DMV
Permit Test Questions

TABLE OF CONTENT

GENERAL PERMIT TEST –

80 Rules and Signs Questions with Explanation

1. UNLESS OTHERWISE STATED, THE SPEED LIMIT FOR A PASSENGER CAR ON A TWO- LANE HIGHWAY IS:
   A. 35 miles per hour
   B. 45 miles per hour
   C. 55 miles per hour
   D. 65 miles per hour

ANSWER C

55 MPH is the maximum speed limit in Massachusetts , and it is still in effect till date.

2. **THE SIGN ABOVE MEANS**
   A. Curve to the right; the highest safe speed is 25 m.p.h.
   B. Curve to the left; drive at least 25 m.p.h.

C. Curve to the left; the highest safe speed is 25 m.p.h.

D. Curve to the right; drive at least 25 m.p.h.

ANSWER A

This road sign curves to the right. It advises drivers against travelling faster than 25 m.p.h.

3. AT AN INTERSECTION OF TWO-WAY STREETS, AFTER COMING TO A FULL STOP AT A RED TRAFFIC LIGHT, A DRIVER MAY:

A. Drive straight ahead if the way is clear

B. Turn left if the way is clear, unless otherwise posted

C. Turn right if the way is clear, unless otherwise posted

D. All of the above

ANSWER C

4. WHAT WOULD YOU DO IF YOU SEE THIS SIGN ABOVE YOUR CAR LANE
   A. May stay in this lane and continue through the interchange
   B. Must exit the freeway if you stay in this lane
   C. May not exit the freeway in this lane
   D. May continue through the interchange or exit the freeway in this lane

ANSWER B

5. THIS YELLOW AND BLACK-DIAMOND SIGN WARNS YOU ABOUT WHAT?
   A. Helps direct you to cities and towns ahead
   B. Tells you about traffic laws and regulations
   C. Warns you about conditions on or near the road
   D. Tells you about road construction ahead

ANSWER C

6. IF YOU WERE INVOLVED IN A CRASH CAUSING DEATH OR PERSONAL INJURY, AND YOU WERE FOUND

GUILTY OF NOT COMING DOWN TO
HELP;
A. Your vehicle must be impounded
B. Your driver's license will be revoked
C. Your insurance will be canceled by the State
D. You will be required to pay the hospital bill

ANSWER B

According to the state of Massachusetts , if you are
found guilty of not stopping to help if your car got
involved in crash that resulted to the death or
injury of someone, your license will be revoked.

7. THIS SIGN ABOVE MEANS WHAT?
A. Trucks under 18,000 lbs. allowed
B. Hill ahead
C. Truck stop ahead
D. No trucks allowed

ANSWER B

This sign warns you of a downgrade or hill up
ahead. It means you are required to slow down and
shift gears to control speed.

8. WHAT DOES THE BROKEN YELLOW CENTER LINE ON A RAOD MEANS?

A. You are in a no passing zone

B. Passing on the left with due care is allowed

C. Reduce your speed ahead

D. No turns are allowed

ANSWER B

Yellow center lines located on a road means you should stick to the right of the line, unless you are overtaking a vehicle in front of you. When you are crossing the yellow line, it should be temporal.

9. THE SIGN ABOVE MEANS?

A. You must turn left or right

B. You are approaching a T-intersection

C. The road that you are on intersects with a divided highway

D. Designates an overpass above a divided highway

ANSWER C

It means that the road on which you are currently driving intersects with a divided highway. It means you can only turn right at the first road, and left at the second.

10. THIS SIGN ABOVE MEANS?
A. Entrance to full parking lots
B. Entrance to road construction areas
C. Entrance to dead-end streets
D. Wrong-way entrance on one-way streets and expressway ramps

ANSWER D

11. IF A SCHOOL BUS STOPS TO UNLOAD CHILDREN ON A TWO-LANE HIGHWAY, VEHICLES TRAVELING IN THE OPPOSITE DIRECTION ARE:
A. Not required to stop

B. Required to signal, then proceed with caution
C. Required to stop, then proceed with caution
D. Required to stop until the stop signal on the bus is withdrawn

ANSWER D

All drivers going either direction of the school bus must remain stopped till the children are cleared off the road.

12. THIS SIGN ABOVE MEANS?
A. No U-Turn
B. No left turn
C. No right turn
D. No turning

ANSWER C

The sign signals you not to make a right turn at the intersection mark.

13. WHEN APPROACHING ANOTHER VEHICLE FROM THE REAR AT NIGHT, YOU MUST DIM YOUR BRIGHT HEADLIGHTS WITHIN:

A. 100 feet of the other vehicle
B. 200 feet of the other vehicle
C. 300 feet of the other vehicle
D. 600 feet of the other vehicle

ANSWER C

When driving behind other vehicles, you should use low beams within 300 feet of the vehicle ahead.

14. THE SIGN ABOVE MEANS

A. A blasting zone
B. An intersection
C. A crosswalk
D. A railroad crossing

ANSWER D

It means a Railroad crossing. This warning sign is usually seen whenever you are approaching highway-rail intercession.

15. BRAKES THAT AUTOMATICALLY STOP A TRAILER IF IT BREAKS AWAY FROM THE TOWING VEHICLE ARE REQUIRED ON ALL TRAILERS EQUAL TO OR EXCEEDING A WEIGHT OF

A. 2,000 pounds
B. 3,000 pounds
C. 5,000 pounds
D. 10,000 pounds

ANSWER B

16. A BROKEN WHITE CENTER LINE ON THE ROADWAY MEANS:

A. No turns are allowed
B. Reduce your speed ahead
C. You are in a no passing zone
D. You may change lanes with due care

Answer D

A broken white line separates two lanes traveling in the same direction. Once you have signaled and if it is safe to do so, you may cross this line when changing lanes.

17.WHENEVER A LOAD EXTENDS TO THE REAR FOUR FEET OR MORE BEYOND THE BED OR BODY OF A VEHICLE IN THE DAYTIME, THE END AND THE SIDE OF THE LOAD MUST BE MARKED BY:
A. White flags
B. Red flags
C. White lights
D. Red lights

ANSWER B

During the day, red flags help notify other drivers of danger. At night, it is safe to use red lights.

18.WHEN DO ROADWAYS BECOME SLIPPERY THE MOST?
A. After it has been raining for awhile
B. During a heavy downpour.
C. The first rain after a dry spell.
Answer C

19. THIS SIGN ABOVE MEANS?
   A. Truck crossing
   B. Road narrows, right lane ends
   C. Divided highway ahead
   D. Hill ahead

ANSWER B

When you see a sign like this, be prepared to change lanes or allow other cars merge into your own lane.

20. THIS SIGN ABOVE MEANS?
   A. All traffic must turn right
   B. Side road
   C. All traffic must go straight ahead
   D. No right turn

ANSWER B

This side road sign enters from the right. It is one of the warning intersections that alerts you on an intersection ahead.

21. WHEN PARKING YOUR VEHICLE FACING UPHILL WITH A CURB, YOU SHOULD POINT YOUR FRONT WHEELS:

A. Into the curb

B. Away from the curb

C. Either into or away from the curb

D. Straight ahead

ANSWER B

Point your front wheels away from the curb when parking your vehicle facing uphill. Don't forget to set the parking brake and place automatic gear shift in park. Shift manual gears to first. If these precautions fail and the vehicle starts rolling, the front wheels will hit the curb and stop the car.

22. IF YOU SEE RED REFLECTORS FACING YOU IN THE PAVEMENT EDGE LINE, THIS MEANS YOU ARE:

A. Approaching a stop sign

B. In a no-passing zone

C. Facing traffic the wrong way

D. Approaching a busy intersection

ANSWER C

If you see red reflectors facing you on the lane lines, you are on the wrong side of the road. Get into the proper lane immediately! Red reflectors always mean you are facing traffic the wrong way and could have a head-on collision.

23. BEFORE YOU REACH THE INTERSECTION, WHEN CROSSING RAILROAD TRACKS IN SLOW TRAFFIC, YOU SHOULD:
   A. Sound your horn as you are crossing the tracks
   B. Stop on the tracks until your light turns green
   C. Stop between the crossing gates in case they close
   D. Wait until you can completely cross the tracks before you proceed

   ANSWER D

24. A DIAMOND-SHAPED SIGN IS A:
   A. Road hazard sign.
   B. Interstate route sign.
   C. School crossing sign.
   D. Speed limit sign.

ANSWER A

The shape of a diamond is reserved exclusively for warning drivers of existing or possible hazards on roadways and adjacent areas. Diamond-shaped signs are either warning signs or work zone traffic signs.

25. WHEN YOU HEAR THE SIREN OR SEE THE FLASHING RED LIGHT OF A CLOSELY APPROACHING EMERGENCY VEHICLE, AND YOU ARE NOT IN THE INTERSECTION, YOU SHOULD:
    A. Drive slowly in the right lane until it has passed
    B. Speed up so that you can stay ahead of it
    C. Drive to the right edge of the road and stop
    D. Choose any of the above options

ANSWER C

26. WHICH OF THESE STATEMENTS IS TRUE ABOUT DRIVING AND TAKING DRUGS?
    A. Only illegal drugs can impair your driving

B. Even over-the-counter drugs can impair your driving
C. Any prescription drug is safe to use if you don't feel drowsy
D. All of the above

ANSWER B

27. WHAT SHOULD BE DONE IF YOU EXPERIENCE BRAKE FAILURE WHILE DRIVING?
    A. Look for an area to slow down and stop after downshifting
    B. Stop off the road and raise an alarm
    C. Keep pumping the brake pedal quickly
    D. Any of the above

    ANSWER D

28. WHEN THE ROAD IS MARKED WITH A SOLID YELLOW LINE AND A BROKEN YELLOW LINE ON YOUR SIDE YOU MAY PASS
    A. Only in an emergency
    B. If you are on an expressway
    C. If traffic is clear
    D. Only at an intersection

    ANSWER C

29. IF YOUR TIRES ARE NOT INFLATED TO
    THE PRESSURE RECOMMENDED BY
    THE MANUFACTURER, IT MAY CAUSE:
    A. Low gas mileage
    B. Uneven tire wear
    C. Improper steering
    D. All of the above

    ANSWER D

30. A RED AND WHITE TRIANGULAR SIGN
    AT AN INTERSECTION MEANS:
    A. Slow down if an emergency vehicle is
       approaching
    B. Look both ways as you cross the intersection
    C. Always come to a full stop at the
       intersection
    D. Slow down and be prepared to stop if
       necessary

ANSWER D

31. WHO IS RESPONSIBLE FOR KNOWING
    HOW YOUR MEDICATIONS AFFECT
    YOUR DRIVING?
    A. You
    B. Your doctor

C. Your pharmacist

D. The DMV clerk

ANSWER A

32. UNLESS OTHERWISE POSTED, THE SPEED LIMIT IN A RESIDENTIAL AREA IS

A. 15 miles per hour

B. 25 miles per hour

C. 30 miles per hour

D. 35 miles per hour

Answer C

Massachusetts Standard speed limits for municipal speed areas, business or residential areas are 30MPH. Speed limit signs are mounted at the entrance of a speed zone. Driver must drive no higher than the stated speed of the posted sign and continue till there is a change of postal speed limit.

33. THIS ROAD SIGN ABOVE MEANS:

A. Pedestrians stay on sidewalk
B. Come to a complete stop ahead
C. School ahead, watch for children
D. Shopping district ahead

Answer C

"The Pentagon shape above is reserved for school signs. This five-sided sign means you are near a school. Therefore you should watch for children."

34. WHEN PASSING A VEHICLE ON A TWO-LANE ROADWAY, YOU MUST RETURN TO RIGHT HAND SIDE OF THE ROAD BEFORE COMING WITHIN

A. 100 feet of an oncoming vehicle
B. 500 feet of an oncoming vehicle
C. 200 feet of an oncoming vehicle
D. 300 feet of an oncoming vehicle

Answer B

Passing is a dangerous maneuver that takes experience and caution. You must have enough space to be able to return to the right side of the road before coming within 200 feet of any incoming vehicle from the opposite direction. At the same time, you should not return to the right side of the road until you can see the tires of the vehicle you passed in your rear view mirror.

35. ON A TWO WAY HIGHWAY, YOU ARE ALLOWED TO DRIVE ON THE LEFT HALF OF THE ROADWAY WHEN

A. There is a double yellow center line
B. It is safe to pass, and passing is allowed
C. You are approaching a corner at which you intend to turn left
D. There is a solid line on your side of the center line

Answer B

On a two-lane way, you are just allowed to drive on the left half of the roadway when it is safe to pass and passing is allowed. If the road has more than four lanes with two-way traffic, you should drive in the right lanes except under the condition of overtaking and passing.

36. A BROKEN WHITE CENTER LINE ON THE ROADWAY MEANS:

E. No turns are allowed
F. Reduce your speed ahead
G. You are in a no passing zone
H. You may change lanes with due care

Answer D

A broken white line separates two lanes traveling in the same direction. Once you have signaled and if it is safe to do so, you may cross this line when changing lanes.

37. THIS SIGN ABOVE MEANS
A. Bicycle rentals are available here
B. Children at play
C. Bikeway crosses roadway, watch for bicycles
D. Park entrance ahead, watch for cars

Answer C

The bicycle crossing sign helps you with an early warning that the road you are traveling on will have a bicycle crossing up ahead. You should Slow down and be on the look-out for cyclists entering and exiting the road. You should also remember the rules of sharing the road with cyclists.

38. THIS SIGN ABOVE MEANS:

A. Crossroad
B. First aid station
C. Church
D. Railroad crossing

Answer A

It means a CROSSROAD. It is the intersection traffic sign.

39. WHEN YOU TOW ANOTHER VEHICLE, THE DRAWBAR BETWEEN

THE VEHICLES MUST NOT BE LONGER THAN

A. 5 feet
B. 10 feet
C. 12 feet
D. 15 feet

Answer D

The connection drawbar mustn't be more than 15 feet unless you are towing pipes, machineries or equipment that cannot be taken apart easily.

40. THIS ROAD SIGN ABOVE MEANS:

A. Stop if traffic is approaching
B. Three-way intersection
C. Crossroad
D. Railroad crossing

Answer D

The above signifies a Railroad crossing, and it is only positioned where tracks cross roads.

41. WHEN APPROACHING A BICYCLIST FROM THE REAR YOU SHOULD SLOW DOWN AND:

A. Wait until it is safe to pass the bicyclist with at least three feet of clearance
B. Tap your horn to warn the bicyclist
C. Follow at least five feet behind the cyclist till it is safe to pass
D. Stay as far as possible in the right lane without hitting the cyclist

Answer A

42. THE SIGN ABOVE MEANS:

A. A Sharp turn to the right
B. Double curve, right then left
C. Double curve, left then right
D. Pavement ends

Answer B

It means a SET OF CURVES from right to left.

43. THE SIGN ABOVE MEANS:
A. Low place in the road
B. Soft shoulders
C. Watch for pedestrians
D. Come to a complete stop

ANSWER A

44. BEFORE MAKING A LEFT OR RIGHT TURN, YOU SHOULD SIGNAL FOR AT LEAST
A. 50 feet
B. 100 feet
C. 300 feet
D. 400 feet

ANSWER B

You should move into the proper lane and signal your turn for the last 100 feet. You may decide to either use the hand signals or mechanical signals.

45. **WHENEVER A LOAD EXTENDS TO THE REAR FOUR FEET OR MORE BEYOND THE BED OR BODY OF A VEHICLE AT NIGHT, THE END AND THE SIDE OF THE LOAD MUST BE MARKED BY:**

A. Four red lamps and two red reflectors
B. Four red flags and two red reflectors
C. Four white lamps and two white reflectors
D. Four white flags and two white reflectors

ANSWER B

The following markers are used at night or in a situation when you can't see clearly: two red lamps on the back of the load which should be seen from at least 500 feet to the rear. Two red reflectors on the rear, which should be seen from at least 100 and 600 feet when directly in front of a low beam headlight.

46. THE SIGN ABOVE MEANS:

A. Turn at the next intersection

B. Divided highway ends

C. One-way street ahead

D. Road closed ahead

ANSWER B

DIVIDED HIGHWAY ENDS.

47. BRAKES THAT AUTOMATICALLY STOP A TRAILER IF IT BREAKS AWAY FROM THE TOWING VEHICLE ARE REQUIRED ON ALL TRAILERS EQUAL TO OR EXCEEDING A WEIGHT OF

E. 2,000 pounds

F. 3,000 pounds

G. 5,000 pounds

H. 10,000 pounds

ANSWER B

48. THE ABOVE SIGN MEANS:
    A. Two-lane road ahead, watch for oncoming vehicles
    B. Road narrows ahead, prepare to merge right
    C. Traffic merges with your lane ahead
    D. Divided highway ahead

ANSWER **C**

It is a MERGING TRAFFIC Sign. Merge signs appear on expressways just before expressway ramps. Drivers entering from the right must yield to traffic on the main route, and must make use of speed-change lanes to merge safely and smoothly with the main traffic flow.

49. A GREEN ARROW SHOWING AT THE SAME TIME AS THE RED TRAFFIC LIGHT MEANS:
    A. Vehicles going in the direction shown by the arrow must stop

B. Do not go in the direction of the arrow until the traffic light turns green
C. You may go in the direction of the arrow with caution
D. Road closed ahead, go in the direction of the arrow

ANSWER **C**

50. **THIS SIGN MEANS**:
    A. Slow down, children at play
    B. Watch for pedestrians crossing the roadway
    C. Pedestrians stay on sidewalk
    D. Come to a complete stop ahead

ANSWER B

PEDESTRIAN CROSSING. You should watch out for people crossing the street. Remember to Slow down or stop if necessary. Remember that people crossing the street on the pedestrian crossing have the right-of-way.

51. IF YOU DRIVE AFTER DRINKING, YOU SHOULD BE AWARE THAT THE FIRST THING ALCOHOL AFFECTS IS:
A. Your hearing
B. Your alertness
C. Your vision
D. Your judgment

ANSWER D

A person's judgment is the first thing affected after drinking any form of alcoholic beverage.

52. WHEN YOU APPROACH A SHARP CURVE IN THE ROAD, YOU SHOULD:
A. Start braking as soon as you enter the curve
B. Start braking before you enter the curve
C. Accelerate into the curve and brake out of it
D. Accelerate through the whole curve to increase traction

ANSWER B

On curves, there is a strong outward pull on your vehicle, which is especially dangerous when the road is slippery. Slow down before you enter the curve; you do not know what may be ahead (stalled car, collision, etc.).

53. WHICH OF THE FOLLOWING IS TRUE ABOUT VEHICLES DISPLAYING A DIAMOND-SHAPED SIGN (INDICATING A HAZARDOUS LOAD)?
   A. They are not allowed to drive on freeways
   B. They are not allowed to exceed 35 mph
   C. They must stop before crossing railroad tracks
   D. They always have the right-of-way

ANSWER C

A diamond-shaped sign on a truck means that the load on the truck is potentially dangerous (gas, explosives, etc.). Police department and fire department officers know what to do if the load is accidentally spilled. Vehicles which display these signs are required to stop before crossing railroad tracks.

54. WHAT ARE THE COLORS OF THE WARNING SIGNS THAT INDICATE

HAZARDS AHEAD, SUCH AS CURVES
IN THE ROAD OR NARROW BRIDGES?
A. Black letters or symbols on a white
   background.
B. Black letters or symbols on a yellow
   background.
C. White letters or symbols on a blue
   background.
D. White letters or symbols on a green
   background.

ANSWER B

55. TURN YOUR FRONT WHEELS TOWARD
    THE CURB WHEN YOU ARE PARKED:
A. Facing uphill
B. On a level road
C. Facing downhill
D. Next to a fire hydrant

ANSWER C

56. WHEN PASSING IN THE ONCOMING
    TRAFFIC LANE OF A TWO LANE ROAD,
    YOU SHOULD CONSIDER:
A. Your speed relative to others, and your
   ability to accelerate
B. How much clear space you need to pass, and
   how much you have

C. The speed and distance of oncoming traffic, and possible hazards

D. All of the above

ANSWER D

57.ORANGE CONSTRUCTION SIGNS WARN YOU:

A. Of workers and road equipment ahead

B. That there are driver services ahead

C. Of an accident ahead

D. That you will have to come to a complete stop shortly

ANSWER A

58.FOLLOWING CLOSELY BEHIND ANOTHER VEHICLE:

A. Helps you avoid other drivers' blind spots

B. Is a common cause of rear-end accidents

C. Increases fuel efficiency

D. Is part of the standard driving test

ANSWER B

59.THE ROAD SURFACE IS MOST SLIPPERY:

A. During a heavy rain or storm

B. Just after the rain

C. Just when it starts raining

D. During a light rain

ANSWER C

60. WHEN YOU ENTER A FREEWAY, YOU
    SHOULD CHECK TRAFFIC BY USING:
A. The inside and outside mirrors only
B. Only your rearview mirrors
C. All mirrors and turning your head
D. Only your left side-view mirror

ANSWER C

61. TEENAGE DRIVERS ARE MORE
    LIKELY TO BE INVOLVED IN A CRASH
    WHEN:
A. They are driving with their peer as a
   passenger
B. They are driving with adult passengers
C. They are driving with teenage passengers
D. They are driving without any passengers

ANSWER C

YOU ARE WAITING AT A RED LIGHT TO
TURN RIGHT, AND A PEDESTRIAN ON
YOUR RIGHT IS WAITING TO CROSS THE
STREET YOU WANT TO ENTER. WHO HAS
THE RIGHT-OF-WAY WHEN YOUR LIGHT
TURNS GREEN?

A. The pedestrian has the right-of-way
B. You have the right-of-way only if the crosswalk is not marked
C. You have the right-of-way because your light is green
D. You have the right-of-way if you move first
   ANSWER A

62. WHAT ARE THE COLORS OF A SIGN WHICH TELLS YOU THE DISTANCE TO THE NEXT EXIT OF A HIGHWAY?
A. Yellow with black letters.
B. Black with white letters.
C. Red with white letters.
D. Green with white letters.

ANSWER D

63. YOU MAY DRIVE ACROSS A SIDEWALK TO:
A. Avoid driving over a speed bump
B. Enter or exit a driveway or alley
C. Make a U-turn
D. Pass a traffic jam

ANSWER B

64. ON THE INTERSECTION, IF YOU SEE A GREEN ARROW POINTING TO THE LEFT, YOU CAN:

A. Go in any direction

B. Make a protected turn left

C. Make a turn left or go straight

D. Turn left only if there are no vehicles coming in the opposite direction

ANSWER B

65. WHEN YOU DRIVE THROUGH AN AREA WHERE CHILDREN ARE PLAYING, YOU SHOULD EXPECT THEM:

A. To know when it is safe to cross

B. To stop at the curb before crossing the street

C. To run our in front of your without looking

D. Not to cross unless they are with an adult

ANSWER C

66. WHEN ROADS ARE SLIPPERY, YOU SHOULD:

A. Decrease the distance you look ahead of your vehicle

B. Stop and test the traction of your tires while going up hills

C. Avoid making fast turns and fast stops

D. Refrain from driving at all costs

ANSWER C

67. WHEN PARKING DOWNHILL AND THE CURB IS ABSENT, YOUR FRONT WHEELS MUST BE TURNED:

A. Towards the road
B. Parallel to the road
C. Towards the side of the road
D. In the direction of traffic

ANSWER C

68. WHEN A TRAFFIC SIGNAL LIGHT IS NOT WORKING, YOU SHOULD:

A. Stop only if other vehicles are present
B. Slow down and stop if necessary
C. Stop and then continue driving when it is safe
D. Proceed through the intersection as usual

ANSWER C

69. IF A PEDESTRIAN IS IN A CROSSWALK IN THE MIDDLE OF A BLOCK:

A. The pedestrian has the right-of-way
B. The pedestrian must yield the right-of-way
C. Vehicles have the right-of-way, but drivers must legally take care for the pedestrian safety

D. Drivers must honk the horn approaching the crosswalk, to urge the pedestrian to cross faster

ANSWER A

70. WHEN MAY YOU LEGALLY DRIVE AROUND OR UNDER A RAILROAD CROSSING GATE?
   A. Under no circumstances
   B. When you can clearly see in both directions
   C. When the gate does not seem to be working correctly
   D. When you think you can drive through before it comes down

ANSWER A

71. THE "THREE-SECOND RULE" APPLIES TO THE SPACE _____ OF YOUR VEHICLE.
   A. to the sides
   B. ahead
   C. in back
   D. all around

ANSWER B

72. IF YOU NEED TO SLOW DOWN OR STOP WHEN OTHER DRIVERS MAY NOT EXPECT IT, YOU SHOULD:
A. Use your emergency brake
B. Look over your shoulder for traffic in your blind spot
C. Quickly tap your brake pedal a few times
D. Get ready to blow your horn

ANSWER C

73. THE CAR BEHIND YOU BEGINS TO PASS YOU. YOU SHOULD
A. Maintain your speed so traffic will flow smoothly
B. Pull to the right and stop so he can pass
C. Slow down slightly and stay in your lane
D. Blow your horn to allow him to pass

ANSWER C

74. IF YOU SEE ORANGE CONSTRUCTION SIGNS AND CONES ON A FREEWAY, YOU MUST:
A. Change lanes and maintain your current speed
B. Be prepared for workers and equipment ahead
C. Slow down because the lane ends ahead

D. Speed up to avoid rubbernecking

ANSWER B

75. WORN OR BALD TIRES:
A. Increase stopping distance, while decreasing overall control
B. Cause vehicles to hydroplane
C. Cause tire failure and/or blown out tires
D. All of the above

ANSWER B

76. DRIVERS WHO EAT AND DRINK WHILE DRIVING:
A. Have no driving errors
B. Have trouble driving slow
C. Are better drivers because they are not hungry
D. Have trouble controlling their vehicles

ANSWER D

77. THIS ROAD SIGN ABOVE MEANS

A. Come to a complete stop ahead
B. School ahead, watch for children
C. Shopping district ahead
D. Pedestrians stay on sidewalk

ANSWER B

77. ON A TWO WAY HIGHWAY, YOU ARE ALLOWED TO DRIVE ON THE LEFT HALF OF THE ROADWAY WHEN

A. There is a double yellow center line
B. There is a solid line on your side of the center line
C. It is safe to pass, and passing is allowed
D. You are approaching a corner at which you intend to turn left

ANSWER C

78. WHEN YOU HEAR THE SIRENS OR SEE THE RED EMERGENCY LIGHTS OF A CLOSELY APPROACHING EMERGENCY VEHICLE, YOU MUST:

A. Speed up to clear traffic
B. Drive slowly until it has passed
C. Drive to the right edge and stop
D. Stop in the intersection

ANSWER C

79. THIS SIGN ABOVE MEANS
   A. Divided highway ahead
   B. One-way traffic ahead
   C. Four-lane highway ahead
   D. Divided highway ends

ANSWER D

80. WHICH OF THE FOLLOWING IS TRUE
   ABOUT VEHICLES DISPLAYING A
   DIAMOND-SHAPED SIGN (INDICATING
   A HAZARDOUS LOAD)?
   E. They are not allowed to drive on freeways
   F. They are not allowed to exceed 35 mph
   G. They must stop before crossing railroad
      tracks
   H. They always have the right-of-way

ANSWER C

TRAFFIC SIGN

65 QUESTIONS and Explanatory Answers

1. You are driving on a one-way street. You may turn left onto another one-way street only if:

   A. A sign permits the turn.

   B. Traffic on the street moves to the right.

   C. Traffic on the street moves to the left.

   Answer C

2. What vehicles must stop at all railroad crossings

   A. Pick up trucks.

   B. School buses and passenger buses carrying passengers.

   C. Motorcycles.

   D. Vehicles towing a trailer.

Answer B

3. You come to an intersection which has a flashing red light. You should

> A. Come to a full stop, then go when safe to do so.
>
> B. Stop only if cars are approaching the intersection.
>
> C. Stop only if cars are already in the intersection.
>
> D. Slow down and be prepared to stop if necessary.

Answer D

4. You see a flashing yellow traffic signal at an upcoming intersection. The flashing yellow light means:

> A. Stop before entering the intersection as long as you can do so safely.
>
> B. Stop. Yield to all cross traffic before crossing the intersection.

C. Slow down and cross the intersection carefully.

Answer C

5. When driving on wet roads, you should:

A. Increase following distance to 5 or 6 seconds

B. Decrease following distance to 2 seconds

C. Not be concerned about following distance

D. Maintain the 4-second following distance rule

Answer A

6. If a vehicle using high beams comes toward you, you should:

A. Turn on your high beams

B. Turn off your headlights

C. Sound your horn

D. Flash your high beams

Answer D

7. Before backing up, you should:

A. Rely on your mirrors to see if it is clear to proceed

B. Flash your lights

C. Open your door to see if it is clear to proceed

D. Turn your head and look through the rear window

Answer D

8. Unless otherwise posted the speed limit in a residential area is ____.

A. 20 mph

B. 25 mph

C. 30 mph

Answer B

9. A rectangular-shaped sign is

A. School crossing sign.

B. Railroad crossing sign.

C. Stop sign.

D. Speed limit sign.

Answer D

10. Which of the following is true about the speed at which you travel?

    A. The safe speed to drive depends on many conditions

    B. Driving slowly is always safer

    C. The speed limit is always a safe speed

    D. Accelerating is always dangerous

    Answer A

11. You may not cross a single broken white (or yellow) line

    A. When to do so would interfere with traffic.

    B. When turning left into a driveway.

    C. When the car in front is disabled.

    D. When passing to the right on a one-way street.

    Answer A

12. To help avoid crashes, you should:

A. Communicate with other drivers on the road

B. Ignore other drivers on the road

C. Drive on side streets and back roads

D. Avoid driving during rush hour

Answer A

13. When driving on slippery roads, you should:

A. Use alternate routes

B. Drive as you would on dry roads

C. Increase your following distance

D. Avoid crossing bridges or intersections

Answer C

You may cross a double, yellow line to pass another vehicle, if the yellow line next to:

A. The other side of the road is a solid line.

B. Your side of the road is a broken line.

C. The other side of the road is a broken line.

Answer B

14. If an approaching train is near enough or going fast enough to be a danger, you must

A. Slow down and proceed with caution.

B. Not cross the tracks until the train has completely passed.

C. Cross the tracks at your own risk.

D. Find an alternative route across tracks.

Answer B

Answer D

15. If a traffic signal light is not working, you must:

A. Stop, then proceed when safe.

B. Stop before entering the intersection and let all other traffic go first.

C. Slow down or stop, only if necessary.

Answer A

16. What can you do to avoid the need to make emergency (or panic) stops while driving in traffic?

A. Honk your horn to make others aware of your presence

B. Look ahead and maintain a safe following distance

C. Drive in the right lane only

D. Drive slower than the flow of traffic

Answer B

17. You are approaching a railroad crossing with no warning devices and are unable to

see 400 feet down the tracks in one direction. The speed limit is:

A. 15 mph

B. 20 mph

C. 25 mph

Answer A

18. If an oncoming driver is heading toward you in your lane, you should:

A. Steer right, blow your horn, and accelerate

B. Steer left, blow your horn, and brake

C. Steer right, blow your horn, and brake

D. Stay in the center of your lane, blow your horn, and brake

Answer C

19. Before passing another vehicle you should:

A. Flash your headlights to alert the driver

B. Turn on your four-way flashers to warn the driver

C. Give the proper turn signal to show you are changing lanes

D. Sound your horn to get the drivers attention

Answer C

20. Before passing another vehicle, you should signal:

A. Just before changing lanes

B. At any time

C. After changing lanes

D. Early enough so others know your plans

Answer D

21. With a Class C drivers license a person may drive:

A. A 3-axle vehicle if the Gross Vehicle Weight is less than 6,000 pounds.

B. Any 3-axle vehicle regardless of the weight.

C. A vehicle pulling two trailers.

Answer A

22. If you are involved in a traffic collision, you are required to complete and submit a written report (SR1) to the DMV:

A. Only if you or the other driver is injured.

B. If there is property damage in excess of $750 or if there are any injuries.

C. Only if you are at fault.

Answer B

23. When you tailgate other drivers (drive close to their rear bumper):

A. You can frustrate the other drivers and make them angry.

B. Your actions cannot result in a traffic citation.

C. You help reduce traffic congestion.

Answer A

24. A traffic light which has a green arrow and a red light means that

    A. You may only drive straight ahead.

    B. You may drive only in the direction of the green arrow.

    C. You must wait for a green light.

    D. Vehicles moving in any direction must stop.

Answer B

25. The amount of space you need to cross traffic depends on the:

    A. Road and weather conditions and oncoming traffic

    B. Presence of a stop sign

    C. Use of your turn signals

    D. Cars behind you

Answer A

26. What are the colors of a sign which tells you the distance to the next exit of a highway

A. Yellow with black letters.

B. Black with white letters.

C. Red with white letters.

D. Green with white letters.

Answer D

27. Drive below the posted speed limit when:

A. Anything makes conditions less than perfect

B. Others drive below the speed limit

C. Entering a highway where there are other cars

D. You are on a four lane road

Answer A

28. The most effective thing you can do to reduce your risk of getting injured or killed in a traffic crash is:

A. Wear your seat belt

B. Limit your driving to week days

C. Stay in the right lane on multi-lane highways

D. Limit your driving to times between 3:00 p.m. and 6:00 p.m.

Answer A

29. What is the appropriate action to take when approaching a railroad crossing that does not have signals (such as lights or crossing gates)

A. Always bring the car to a complete stop.

B. Slow down and be prepared to stop.

C. Do nothing; all railroad crossings have signals.

D. Increase speed to get across the tracks quickly.

Answer B

30. A solid white line on the right edge of the highway slants in towards your left. That shows that

A. There is an intersection just ahead.

B. You are approaching a construction area.

C. You will be required to turn left just ahead.

D. The road will get narrower.

Answer D

31. When traveling below 40 miles per hour on a limited access highway, you should:

A. Drive on the shoulder

B. Use your high beams

C. Sound your horn to warn others

D. Use your four-way flashers

Answer D

32. Your brake lights tell other drivers that you:

A. Are making a turn

B. Have your emergency brake on

C. Are changing lanes

D. Are slowing down or stopping

Answer D

33. You may cross a double solid yellow line

       A. To pass a slow moving truck.

       B. To turn into a driveway.

       C. To pass a car if traffic permits.

       D. Under no conditions.

Answer B

34. You may honk your horn when you:

       A. Have to stop quickly

       B. Are passing another car

       C. Have lost control of your car

       D. Are passing a bicyclist

Answer A

35. You must obey instructions from school crossing guards:

       A. At all times.

       B. Only during school hours.

C. Unless you do not see any children present.

Answer A

36. You may cross a single solid white line in the highway

A. Whenever you want to.

B. If traffic conditions require.

C. Only to turn into a driveway.

D. Only to make a u-turn.

Answer B

37. What does a flashing yellow light mean

A. Merging traffic.

B. Proceed with caution.

C. Pedestrian crossing.

D. Come to a full stop.

Answer B

38. You are driving on a freeway posted for 65 MPH. The traffic is traveling at 70 MPH. You may legally drive:

A. 70 mph or faster to keep up with the speed of traffic.

B. Between 65 mph and 70 mph.

C. No faster than 65 mph.

Answer C

39. If traffic prevents you from crossing all the way across a set of railroad tracks, you may proceed only when

A. An approaching train is not moving fast enough to be a danger.

B. There is room for your vehicle on the other side.

C. At least one-half of your vehicle can cross the tracks.

D. No trains are in sight.

Answer B

40. If you need to slow down or stop when other drivers may not expect it, you should:

A. Quickly tap your brake pedal a few times

B. Use your emergency brake

C. Look over your shoulder for traffic in your blind spot

D. Get ready to blow your horn

Answer A

41. At highway speeds, on a dry road, a safe following distance is at least:

A. 3 seconds of following distance from the car ahead of you

B. 2 seconds of following distance from the car ahead of you

C. 4 seconds of following distance from the car ahead of you

D. 2 car lengths of following distance from the car ahead of you

Answer C

42. Your blind spot is the area of the road:

A. You cannot see without moving your head

B. Directly behind your vehicle

C. You see in your rearview mirror

D. You see in your side mirror

Answer A

43. When driving on wet roads, you should:

A. Drive the speed limit

B. Drive slightly faster than the speed limit

C. Drive 5 to 10 miles below the speed limit

D. Stay close to the vehicle ahead

Answer C

44. A diamond-shaped sign is a

A. Road hazard sign.

B. Interstate route sign.

C. School crossing sign.

D. Speed limit sign.

Answer A

45. You see a signal person at a road construction site ahead. You should obey his or her instructions:

       A. Only if you see orange cones on the road ahead.

       B. Unless they conflict with existing signs, signals, or laws.

       C. At all times.

       Answer C

46. To prepare for anything coming up in the road ahead, you should:

       A. Continually scan the entire road and roadsides

       B. Stare straight ahead at all times

       C. Drive with your left foot resting lightly on the brake pedal

       D. Maintain focus toward the middle of the road

       Answer A

47. You must use your headlights when other vehicles are not visible from _____ feet away.

 A. 1000

 B. 1500

 C. 1800

 D. 1200

 Answer A

48. When driving on slick roads, you should:

 A. Take turns more slowly

 B. Change lanes quickly

 C. Accelerate quickly

 D. Brake hard

 Answer A

49. If the rear of your vehicle starts to skid left, you should:

 A. Steer left

 B. Hit your brakes

 C. Accelerate

D. Steer right

Answer A

50. Before changing lanes on a multi-lane highway you should:

A. Sound your horn

B. Turn on your headlights

C. Reduce your speed

D. Check your mirrors and blind spots

Answer D

51. An intersection has a stop sign, crosswalk, but no stop line. You must stop

A. Before the crosswalk.

B. 50 feet before the intersection.

C. Where you think the stop line would be.

D. With your front wheels in the crosswalk.

Answer A

52. Which of the following must you obey over the other three

    A. A steady red light.

    B. A policeman.

    C. A stop sign.

    D. A flashing red light.

    Answer B

53. Which of these vehicles must always stop before crossing railroad tracks?

    A. Tank trucks marked with hazardous materials placards.

    B. Motor homes or pickup trucks towing a boat trailer.

    C. Any vehicle with 3 or more axles or weighing more than 4,000 pounds.

    Answer A

54. When the road is marked with a solid yellow line and a broken yellow line on your side you may pass

    A. Only in an emergency.

B. If you are on an expressway.

C. If traffic is clear.

D. Only at an intersection.

Answer C

55. If a vehicle using high beams comes toward you, you should look towards _____ of the road.

A. Either side

B. The center

C. The right side

D. The left side

Answer C

56. Before turning, you should:

A. Use your signal

B. Turn the wheel

C. Increase your speed

D. Change lanes

Answer A

57. If your turn signals fail, you should use _____ to indicate you are turning.

    A. Your horn

    B. Your headlights

    C. Hand signals

    D. Your emergency flashers

    Answer C

58. Should you always drive slower than other traffic?

    A. No, you can block traffic when you drive too slowly.

    B. Yes, it is a good defensive driving technique.

    C. Yes, it is always safer than driving faster than other traffic.

    Answer A

59. As you near an intersection, the traffic light changes from green to yellow. Your best action would be to

    A. Speed up to beat the red light.

B. Apply the brakes sharply to stop.

C. Be prepared to stop in the center of the intersection.

D. Be prepared to stop before the intersection.

Answer D

60. The safest precaution that you can take regarding the use of cellular phones and driving is:

A. Use hands-free devices so you can keep both hands on the steering wheel.

B. Keep your phone within easy reach so you won't need to take your eyes off the road.

C. Review the number before answering a call.

Answer A

61. You should honk your horn when you:

A. Are travelling through an intersection

B. Are passing a bicyclist

C. See a child who is about to run into the street

D. Are parallel parking

Answer C

62. When you park on the roadway, you should:

A. Use your four-way flashers

B. Park at an angle

C. Keep your turn signal on

D. Turn your lights on

Answer A

63. You just sold your vehicle. You must notify the DMV within _____ days.

A. 5

B. 10

C. 15

Answer B

64. Which of the following is used on some highways to direct drivers into the proper lanes for turning

    A. Flashing red lights.

    B. Flashing yellow lights.

    C. White lines on the side of the road.

    D. White arrows in the middle of the lanes.

    Answer D

65. Your ability to stop is affected by:

    A. Signal lights

    B. Other cars on the road

    C. The time of day

    D. The condition of the road

    Answer D

DRUGS AND ALCOHOL

40 PRACTICE QUESTIONS

1. ACUTE CAUSES OF ALCOHOL-RELATED DEATHS ARE LED BY TRAFFIC COLLISIONS, FOLLOWED BY _____.
   - A. homicides and drug toxicity
   - B. suicides and falls
   - C. homicides and suicides
   - D. falls and drug toxicity

ANSWER C

2. FOR WHAT REASON IS IT RECOMMENDED TO TILT YOUR STEERING WHEEL DOWNWARD, IF IT IS ADJUSTABLE?
   - A. To point the air bag towards your chest instead of your head
   - B. To create better leverage for steering
   - C. To increase your distance from the air bag
   - D. To remove it from your view of the road

ANSWER A

3. WHICH OF THE FOLLOWING BEST
   DESCRIBES WHO MUST ACCOMPANY
   THE LEARNER FOR LEGAL USE OF A
   LEARNERS LICENSE?
   A. A person with at least an Intermediate
      license
   B. A family member
   C. A licensed driver at least 21 years old in the
      front passenger seat
   D. A licensed driver at least 21 years old in any
      seat

ANSWER C

4. ACCORDING TO THE FINANCIAL
   RESPONSIBILITY LAW, IF YOU ARE THE
   OWNER OR OPERATOR OF A VEHICLE
   AND YOU ARE AT FAULT IN A
   COLLISION, YOU MAY BE REQUIRED TO
   _____ BEFORE YOUR DRIVING
   PRIVILEGE IS RESTORED.
   A. pay for the damages
   B. pass a driving test
   C. pay a fine
   D. take a traffic school course

ANSWER A

5. IN 2007, THE TWO MOST COSTLY
COMPONENTS OF UNDERAGE DRINKING
IN MASSACHUSETTS WERE

_____.

A. violent crime and drug toxicity deaths
B. violent crime and traffic collisions
C. drug toxicity deaths and rehabilitation
D. None of the above

ANSWER B

6. HOW MUCH ALCOHOL CAN YOU
CONSUME AND STILL EXPECT TO BE
ABLE TO DRIVE SAFELY?
A. None
B. Half a drink
C. One drink
D. Two drinks

ANSWER A

7. _____ SEPARATING LANES
MEANS THAT CHANGING LANES IS
HIGHLY DISCOURAGED FOR SAFETY
REASONS.
A. Reflective markers
B. One solid white line
C. One broken yellow line
D. One broken white line

ANSWER B

8. A CURB OF THIS COLOR MEANS YOU MAY NOT STOP.
   A. Yellow
   B. Green
   C. Red
   D. Blue

ANSWER C

9. WHICH OF THE FOLLOWING IS RECOMMENDED AS A WAY TO PREVENT VEHICLE BACKOVER DEATHS?
   A. Do not allow children to play in driveways
   B. Roll down your windows
   C. Look behind you the entire time you're backing up
   D. All of the above

ANSWER D

10. THE SHORT-TERM EFFECTS OF MARIJUANA INCLUDE _____.
   A. loss of coordination
   B. sleepiness
   C. increased heart rate
   D. All of the above

ANSWER D

11. WHICH OF THE FOLLOWING TYPES OF
EMOTIONAL DISTRESS IS NOT
DANGEROUS WHILE DRIVING?
A. Anger
B. Sadness
C. Impatience
D. None of the above

ANSWER D

12. YOU ARE NOT GUILTY OF DUI IF YOU
ARE DRIVING IN AN UNSAFE MANNER
AFTER DRINKING TOO MUCH COFFEE.
A. TRUE
B. FALSE

ANSWER B

13. IF YOU ARE DRIVING WHILE IMPAIRED,
COMMIT MANSLAUGHTER OR
VEHICULAR HOMICIDE, AND LEAVE
THE SCENE OF THE CRIME, YOU WILL
BE _____.
A. fined up to $1,000 and imprisoned for up to
5 years
B. fined up to $5,000 and imprisoned for up to
10 years

C. fined up to $10,000 and imprisoned for up to 15 years

D. fined up to $10,000 and imprisoned for up to 30 years

ANSWER D

14. YOU SHOULD HAVE YOUR BATTERY AND CHARGING SYSTEM CHECKED _____.

A. at least once a year

B. no more than once a year

C. at least twice a year

D. no more than twice a year

ANSWER A

15. IN 2009, ROUGHLY _____ OF HEAVY DRINKERS AGE 12 OR OLDER WERE CURRENT USERS OF ILLEGAL DRUGS.

A. 13%

B. 20%

C. 33%

D. 50%

ANSWER C

16. WHICH OF THE FOLLOWING IS A CONSEQUENCE OF CHRONIC ALCOHOL USE?
   A. Gastritis
   B. Stomach ulcers
   C. Heartburn
   D. All of the above

ANSWER D

17. _____ ARE AN INDICATION THAT YOUR VEHICLE MAY BE DEVELOPING A COOLING SYSTEM PROBLEM.
   A. Abrupt changes or trends in engine temperature
   B. Foggy windows
   C. Squeaking brakes
   D. Low temperatures in the cabin

ANSWER A

18. WHICH OF THE FOLLOWING IS NOT A REASON THAT YOUNG PEOPLE ARE ESPECIALLY LIKELY TO ABUSE ALCOHOL AND DRUGS?
   A. Their organs are more vulnerable to alcohol
   B. They have more opportunities to consume alcohol

C. They haven't developed healthier ways to cope
D. They don't know how their bodies will react when they drink

ANSWER B

19. HARMFUL EFFECTS OF PAIN RELIEVERS INCLUDE _____.
   A. excessive buildup of stomach lining
   B. liver damage and thickening of the blood
   C. liver damage, thinning of the blood, and over-sensitivity to light
   D. None of the above

ANSWER C

20. YOU MAY OBTAIN AN INTERMEDIATE LICENSE IF YOU HAVE HELD A LEARNERS LICENSE FOR SIX MONTHS WITHOUT RECEIVING ANY TRAFFIC CONVICTIONS.
   A. TRUE
   B. FALSE

ANSWER A

21._____ IS THE ACT OF DECLARING A DRIVERS LICENSE VOID AND TERMINATED WHEN IT IS DETERMINED THAT THE LICENSE WAS ISSUED THROUGH ERROR OR FRAUD.

A. Revocation

B. Suspension

C. Cancellation

D. Restriction

ANSWER C

22._____ IS OFTEN THE FIRST DRUG MANY PEOPLE ABUSE.

A. Cocaine

B. Dextromethorphan

C. Vicodin

D. Alcohol

ANSWER D

23. ALCOHOLIC CARDIOMYOPATHY IS ESPECIALLY DANGEROUS BECAUSE _____.

A. blood can leak from the heart into the chest cavity

B. it can be passed to infants through the parents' genes
C. sufferers sometimes show no symptoms until a fatal heart attack
D. All of the above

ANSWER C

24. WHEN THE LIVER AND KIDNEYS ARE OVERBURDENED BY CHRONIC ALCOHOL USE, THEY CAN INCREASE _____

A. the rate of metabolism of nutrients
B. the production of white blood cells
C. the amount of harmful substances released into the bloodstream
D. A and C

ANSWER C

25. THE PENALTIES FOR A FIRST-TIME DUI CHARGE INCLUDE REVOCATION OF DRIVERS LICENSE FOR _____.
A. 180 days
B. between 180 days and one year
C. between 90 and 180 days
D. one year

ANSWER B

26. INHALANTS INCLUDE CHEMICALS
FOUND IN _____.

    A. shampoo and conditioner
    B. paint thinners, lighter fluid, and glue
    C. whipped cream spray bottles
    D. B and C

ANSWER D

27. WHAT IS THE MAXIMUM FINE
    PERMITTED FOR A FOURTH DUI
    CONVICTION?
    A. 10000
    B. 20000
    C. 50000
    D. There is no maximum fine for a fourth DUI
       conviction.

ANSWER D

28. _____ HAVE EFFECTS SIMILAR TO
    THOSE OF LSD, BUT WITH STRONGER
    EFFECTS OF DULLED SENSES, LOSS OF
    SENSE OF SELF, AND SEDATION.
    A. Antihistamines
    B. Barbiturates
    C. Dissociatives
    D. Opioids

ANSWER C

29. WHICH OF THE FOLLOWING IS A
    MOTOR VEHICLE ACCORDING TO
    MASSACHUSETTS LAW?
    A. A bicycle
    B. A motorized bicycle
    C. A motorized wheelchair
    D. A school bus

ANSWER D

30. THE _____ BREAKS DOWN COMPLEX
    MOLECULES INTO SIMPLER PARTS AND
    ALLOWS THEM TO BE CARRIED OUT OF
    THE BODY AS WASTE.
    A. pancreas
    B. bladder
    C. liver
    D. none of the above

ANSWER C

31. THE EFFECT OF ALCOHOL ON THE
    HUMAN BODY IS TO _____.
    A. cause feelings of happiness
    B. cause feelings of pleasure
    C. slow down bodily functions until eventually
       they stop

D. increase heart rate

ANSWER C

32. EFFECTS OF CHRONIC _____
USE INCLUDE EMPHYSEMA, HEART
DISEASE, STROKE, IMPOTENCE,
INFERTILITY, STRESS, AND CANCER OF
NUMEROUS ORGANS.
A. tobacco
B. heroin
C. cocaine
D. alcohol

ANSWER A

33. IF YOU PROVIDED FALSE
INFORMATION IN YOUR DRIVERS
LICENSE APPLICATION, YOUR LICENSE
WILL BE _____.
A. revoked
B. suspended
C. cancelled
D. restricted

ANSWER C

34. WHEN DRINKING AT A PRIVATE
EVENT, YOU SHOULD ASSUME THAT
DRINKS WILL _____.

A. be stronger than normal

B. be weaker than normal

C. not consistently have the same strength

D. be made with unusual liquors

ANSWER C

35. IMPAIRED DRIVERS OFTEN _____
WITHOUT CHECKING FOR CROSS
TRAFFIC OR PEDESTRIANS.
A. stare straight ahead
B. scan the road ahead
C. obey almost all traffic laws
D. None of the above

ANSWER A

36. IT IS ILLEGAL TO MODIFY YOUR
_____ SYSTEM OR INSTALL A
BYPASS DEVICE TO INCREASE THE
NOISE LEVEL OF YOUR VEHICLE.
A. cooling
B. exhaust
C. evaporative emissions
D. None of the above

ANSWER B

37. A CITATION FOR DRIVING 16 MPH OR
MORE OVER THE LAWFUL SPEED LIMIT

PUTS _____ POINTS ON YOUR
LICENSE.
A. 2
B. 3
C. 4
D. 5

ANSWER C

38.IN WHICH OF THE FOLLOWING CASES
IS AN INTERMEDIATE LICENSED
DRIVER NOT PERMITTED TO DRIVE?
A. He or she is age 16 and the time is 11:15
p.m.
B. A licensed driver age 23 is in the front
passenger seat.
C. He or she is driving to work.
D. He or she is age 17 and the time is 12:45
a.m.

ANSWER A

39.HEROIN AND COCAINE DON'T AFFECT
YOUR PHYSICAL COORDINATION IN
EXACTLY THE SAME WAYS AS
ALCOHOL, _____.
A. so they are less dangerous when driving
B. but you will still be unable to drive safely
C. and cocaine actually improves coordination

D. but dextromethorphan does

ANSWER B

40. WHICH OF THE FOLLOWING BEST DESCRIBES WHO MUST ACCOMPANY THE LEARNER FOR LEGAL USE OF A LEARNERS LICENSE?
   E. A person with at least an Intermediate license
   F. A family member
   G. A licensed driver at least 21 years old in the front passenger seat
   H. A licensed driver at least 21 years old in any seat

ANSWER C

ROAD SIGN QUESTIONS

70 QUESTIONS WITH ANSWERS AND EXPLANATIONS

1. This warning sign means?

> A. Left curve ahead warning.
>
> B. Merging traffic from the right.
>
> C. Hairpin curve ahead, extreme right curve.
>
> D. Right turn ahead warning.
>
> Answer C

2. This warning sign means?

> A. Right lane stays to the right, left lane stays to the left.

B. Keep to the right, merging traffic ahead.

C. Keep to the left, merging traffic ahead.

D. Traffic is permitted to pass on either side of an island or obstruction.

Answer D

3. This sign means?

A. Highway exit only.

B. One lane traffic, keep to the right.

C. Traffic is prohibited from entering a restricted roadway.

D. Road closed, construction ahead.

Answer C

4. This road sign means:

A. No U-turn.

B. Curve.

C. Turn right or left.

D. Traffic flows only in the direction of the arrow.

Answer D

5. This sign means

A. Divided highway ahead.

B. One-way traffic ahead.

C. Four-lane highway ahead.

D. Divided highway ends.

6. This warning sign means?

A. Right lane stays to the right, left lane stays to the left.

B. Keep to the right, merging traffic ahead.

C. Keep to the left, merging traffic ahead.

D. Traffic is permitted to pass on either side of an island or obstruction.

Answer D

7. What type of sign is this?

A. State route sign.

B. U. S. route sign.

C. County route sign.

D. Interstate route sign.

Answer B

8. This sign means?

A. General information sign for a library.

B. General information sign for a bus stop.

C. General information sign for a school.

D. General information sign for a park.

Answer A

9. This sign means?

A. No motor vehicles allowed.

B. No pedestrian crossing.

C. Pedestrian crossing.

D. School crossing.

Answer D

10. This warning sign means?

A. Winding road ahead.

B. The road ahead curves sharply right, then left.

C. The road ahead turns sharply left.

D. The road ahead curves sharply left, then right.

Answer B

11. This sign means

A. Slow down if an emergency vehicle is approaching.

B. Look both ways as you cross the intersection.

C. Always come to a full stop at the intersection.

D. Slow down and be prepared to stop if necessary.

Answer D

12. This sign means?

A. No left turn.

B. No u-turn.

C. No right turn.

D. No turn on red.

Answer A

13. This sign means?

A. Merging traffic from the right.

B. Winding road, use caution.

C. Slippery when wet, use caution.

D. Sharp left curve then right curve, use caution.

Answer C

14. This road sign means:

A. Right lane ends soon, merge left.

B. Soft shoulders.

C. Low place in the road.

D. Lane ends soon, merge right

Answer A

15. This sign means

A. Continue at your current speed.

B. You must stop ahead.

C. Speeding is not allowed.

D. There is a traffic signal ahead.

Answer D

16. This sign means?

A. Maximum legal speed is 50 mph in ideal conditions.

B. Maximum legal speed is 50 mph in all weather conditions.

C. Minimum legal speed is 50 mph in ideal conditions.

D. Minimum legal speed is 50 mph in all weather conditions.

Answer A

17. This sign means

A. One-way traffic

B. Intersection ahead.

C. Merging traffic from the right.

D. Highway curves ahead.

Answer C

18. This sign means?

A. Advance warning of a low speed sharp left curve.

B. Road curves right, then turns left.

C. Advance warning of a winding road.

D. Advance warning of a right curve.

Answer A

19. A white painted curb means:

A. Loading zone for freight or passengers.

B. Loading zone for passengers or mail only.

C. Loading zone for freight only.

Answer B

20. This warning sign means.

A. Reverse curve ahead.

B. One-way traffic ahead.

C. A divided highway ends ahead.

D. A divided highway begins ahead.

Answer C

21. What type of sign is this?

A. State route sign.

B. U. S. route sign.

C. County route sign.

D. Interstate route sign.

Answer C

22. This sign means?

A. Warning sign for truck ramp.

B. Warning sign for draw bridge ahead.

C. Warning sign for hill ahead.

D. No trucks warning sign.

Answer C

23. This sign means?

A. Warning of divided highway ends ahead.

B. Warning of divided highway begins ahead.

C. Two way traffic advance warning.

D. Winding road advance warning.

Answer B

24. This sign means?

A. Route H highway sign.

B. General service sign for a highway.

C. General service sign for a hotel.

D. General service sign for a hospital.

Answer D

25. This sign means

A. Trucks under 18,000 lbs. allowed.

B. Hill ahead.

C. Truck stop ahead.

D. No trucks allowed

Answer B

26. This warning sign means?

A. This road or street terminates ahead.

B. Do not enter, wrong way.

C. Two-way traffic ends ahead.

D. Wrong way, turn around.

Answer A

27. This sign means?

A. Come to a complete stop, proceed only when safe to do so.

B. Slow down and yield to oncoming traffic

C. Stop only to avoid an accident

D. Slow down and proceed if traffic allows.

Answer A

28. What type of sign is this?

A. Interstate route sign.

B. County route sign.

C. State route sign.

D. U. S. route sign.

Answer A

29. This sign means?

A. General information sign for an aircraft manufacturing plant.

B. No fly zone ahead.

C. General information sign for an airport.

D. Low flying aircraft warning.

Answer C

30. The correct hand signal for stopping is:

A. Right hand and arm pointing downward.

B. Left hand and arm pointing straight out.

C. Left hand and arm pointing downward.

D. Left hand and arm pointing upward.

Answer C

31. This sign means?

A. T-Road intersection ahead.

B. A two-way intersection ahead.

C. A four-way intersection ahead.

D. Side road intersection ahead.

Answer C

32. This sign means?

A. Narrow bridge warning.

B. Merging traffic from the right.

C. Left lane ends ahead.

D. Soft shoulder warning.

Answer A

33. This sign means?

A. Max speed 50 mph, minimum speed 30 mph in all conditions.

B. Speed limit is 50 mph, minimum fine of $50 for violations.

C. Max speed 50 mph, minimum speed 30 mph in ideal conditions.

D. Speed limit is 50 mph, minimum fine of $30 for violations.

Answer C

34. This warning sign means?

A. Winding road ahead, begins with a curve to the right.

B. The road curves to the left then to the right.

C. Winding road ahead, begins with a curve to the left.

D. Slippery when wet.

Answer A

35. This road sign means:

A. You may turn during the red light.

B. Pass only in the right lane.

C. One way street.

D. Do not turn during the red light.

Answer A

36. This sign means?

A. U-turn is prohibited.

B. No left lane.

C. Left lane ends.

D. No left turn.

Answer A

37. This sign means?

A. Two way traffic warning.

B. Warning for 2 lane highway.

C. Left lane ends ahead.

D. Right lane ends ahead.

Answer D

38. This sign means

A. Merging traffic is approaching from the right.

B. Winding road ahead.

C. Right lane ends ahead, stay to the left.

D. Divided highway ahead.

Answer C

39. This sign means?

A. No playing in the street.

B. No parking allowed.

C. No passing allowed.

D. No pedestrian traffic.

Answer B

40.This warning sign means?

A. U-turns allowed ahead.

B. Left curve ahead.

C. Circular intersection ahead.

D. Three-way intersection ahead.

Answer C

41.This warning sign means?

A. Road striping ahead.

B. Utility crew ahead.

C. Children`s playground ahead.

D. Road maintenance crew ahead.

Answer C

42. This road sign means:

A. Warning of a hazard.

B. Yield right-of-way.

C. Railroad crossing.

D. Speed limit.

Answer A

43. This sign means?

A. Four-way intersection ahead.

B. Side road intersection ahead.

C. Intersection warning ahead,
roadway ends, must turn right or left.

D. Y intersection ahead.

Answer C

44. This sign means?

A. Warning that a stop sign is ahead.

B. Forward traffic is not allowed.

C. Wrong way, do not enter.

D. A warning to stop right away.

Answer A

45. This sign means?

A. A sharp left curve warning.

B. A sharp right curve or turn.

C. V intersection ahead.

D. 2 Lane traffic ahead.

Answer B

46. This warning sign means?

A. Pavement ends ahead.

B. Lane ends ahead.

C. Road construction ahead.

D. Road closed ahead.

Answer A

47. This sign means?

A. Warning of a winding road ahead.

B. Warning of a right curve ahead.

C. Warning of merging traffic to the right.

D. Warning of a right turn ahead.

Answer B

48. If you see orange construction signs and cones on a freeway, you must:

A. Slow down because the lane ends ahead.

B. Be prepared for workers and equipment ahead.

C. Change lanes and maintain your current speed.

Answer B

49. This sign means

A. All traffic turn left.

B. No left turn.

C. No U-turn.

D. Truck route to the left.

Answer B

50. This sign means

A. Don't drink if you are going to drive.

B. Slippery when wet.

C. Road curves ahead.

D. You are approaching a hill.

Answer B

51. This warning sign means?

A. Pavement ends ahead.

B. Ahead is a sharp depression in the profile of the road.

C. Ahead is a narrow bridge warning.

D. Ahead is a sharp rise in the profile of the road.

Answer B

52. This road sign means:

A. Church.

B. First aid station.

C. Four-way intersection.

D. Railroad crossing.

Answer C

53. This sign means?

A. No hunting allowed.

B. Wildlife reserve area.

C. Deer crossing ahead.

D. State park area.

Answer C

54.This sign means?

A. No u-turn.

B. No right turn.

C. No turn on red.

D. No left turn.

Answer B

55.Two sets of solid, double, yellow lines that are two or more feet apart:

A. May be crossed to enter or exit a private driveway.

B. May not be crossed for any reason.

C. Should be treated as a separate traffic lane.

Answer B

56. This sign means?

A. A flagger is stationed ahead to control road users.

B. End of road construction.

C. Road construction detour to the left.

D. Road construction detour to the right.

Answer A

57. This sign means?

A. General service sign for a hospital.

B. General service sign for a doctor's office.

C. General service sign for a pharmacy.

D. General service sign for parking.

Answer C

58. This warning sign means?

A. Merging traffic entering from the left.

B. Merging traffic entering from the right.

C. Two lane traffic ahead.

D. Intersection warning ahead.

Answer A

59. What does this sign mean?

A. A truck is 500 feet ahead of you.

B. Slow down for the truck ahead.

C. A farm vehicle, or tractor, is 500 feet ahead of you.

D. Caution and keep a 500 foot distance between yourself and the farm vehicle ahead of you.

Answer D

60. This sign means?

A. No parking anytime.

B. Disabled parking spot.

C. No parking here to the corner.

D. No stopping or standing.

Answer B

61. This sign means?

A. Divided highway ends.

B. Wrong way, turn around.

C. Traffic flows only in the direction of the arrow.

D. Divided highway begins.

Answer C

62. This sign means?

A. Divided highway ends.

B. Keep to the right of obstruction.

C. Keep to the left of obstruction.

D. Left lane ends.

Answer B

63. This sign means?

A. Highway exit only.

B. One lane traffic, keep to the right.

C. Traffic is prohibited from entering a restricted roadway.

D. Road closed, construction ahead.

Answer C

64. This sign means?

A. Right curve warning ahead.

B. Merging traffic entering from the left.

C. Merging traffic entering from the right.

D. 2 Lane traffic ahead.

Answer C

65. This sign means?

    A. Pedestrians only, no vehicle traffic.

    B. School advance warning, you are entering a school zone.

    C. Pedestrian crossing ahead.

    D. Pedestrians ahead warning sign.

    Answer B

66. This warning sign means?

    A. Road ramp ahead.

    B. Low clearance ahead.

    C. Road narrows ahead.

    D. Road under water ahead.

Answer B

67. This sign means?

A. Traffic flows only to the right.

B. Traffic flows only to the left.

C. Your lane will end ahead.

D. Do not drive past this sign, turn around.

Answer D

68. What type of sign is this?

A. U. S. route sign.

B. County route sign.

C. State route sign.

D. Interstate route sign.

Answer C

69. This sign means?

A. Completely stop at sign and yield right-of-way traffic.

B. Slow down for an approaching intersection.

C. Slow down, completely stop if required, yield right-of-way traffic.

D. Wrong way, do not enter.

Answer C

70. This sign means?

A. Church crossing.

B. Pedestrian crossing.

C. Pedestrian traffic only.

D. School crossing.

Answer D

DEFENSIVE DRIVING

50 QUESTIONS WITH EXPLANATORY ANSWERS

1. When sharing the road with a truck, it is important to remember that, in general, trucks:

   A. Take longer distances than cars to stop

   B. Require less time to pass on a downgrade than cars

   C. Require less turning radius than cars

   D. Require less time to pass on an incline than cars

   Answer A

2. When entering a freeway:

   A. Vehicles on the freeway must always yield the right-of-way to vehicles that are entering the freeway.

B. You must yield the right-of-way to vehicles already on the freeway.

C. Increase your speed even if the way is not clear.

D. You must always drive at the same speed as the rest of the traffic.

Answer B

3. When driving on a freeway entrance ramp, you should look for a gap in freeway traffic by:

A. Looking in the inside rearview mirror only

B. Looking in the sideview mirror only

C. Looking in both rearview and sideview mirrors

D. Looking in your mirrors and turning your head to look over your shoulder

Answer D

4. You need to use extra caution when driving near a pedestrian using a white cane because:

    A. He or she is deaf

    B. He or she has a mental disability

    C. He or she is blind

    D. He or she has a walking problem

    Answer C

5. At night, it is hardest to see:

    A. Road signs

    B. Pedestrians

    C. Other motorists

    D. Street lights

    Answer B

6. The four-second rule refers to how one should:

    A. Yield to other cars

    B. Turn at stop signs

    C. Follow another car

D. Cross an intersection

Answer C

7. U-turns in residential districts are legal:

A. On a one-way street on a green arrow.

B. When there are no vehicles approaching nearby.

C. Across two sets of solid double, yellow lines.

Answer B

8. The only time you do not have to stop for a school bus whose red lights are flashing and stop arm is extended is when you:

A. Are driving on the opposite side of a divided highway

B. Are behind the bus

C. See no children present

D. Can safely pass on the left

Answer A

9. The law gives _____ the right of way at intersections.

   A. No one

   B. Drivers turning left

   C. Drivers going straight

   D. Drivers turning right

   Answer A

10. Seat belts can be most effective as injury preventive devices when they are worn by

    A. The person driving the car.

    B. Passengers when they are on a long drive.

    C. All occupants of a car being driven on an expressway.

    D. Passengers and the driver whenever they are in the car.

    Answer D

11. When exiting a highway, you should slow down:

A. On the main road, just before the exit lane

B. Once you see the toll booth

C. Once you have moved into the exit lane

D. When you first see the exit sign

Answer C

12. You can park and leave your car

A. In a tunnel.

B. 30 feet from a railroad crossing.

C. Between a safety zone and the curb.

D. None of the above.

Answer D

13. When a school bus has its lights flashing and its stop arm extended, you must:

A. Stop at least 10 feet away from the bus

B. Pass if children have exited the bus

C. Stop if the bus is on the opposite side of a barrier

D. Drive slowly by the bus

Answer A

14. Drivers who eat and drink while driving:

A. Have no driving errors

B. Have trouble driving slow

C. Are better drivers because they are not hungry

D. Have trouble controlling their vehicles

Answer D

15. When passing a bicyclist, you should:

A. Blast your horn to alert the bicyclist

B. Move as far left as possible

C. Remain in the center of the lane

D. Put on your four-way flashers

Answer B

16. Who must yield when a driver is turning and a pedestrian is crossing without a traffic light?

    A. Whoever started last

    B. The driver

    C. Whoever is slower

    D. The pedestrian

    Answer B

17. To turn left on multi-lane streets and highways, you should start from:

    A. The middle of the intersection

    B. The right lane

    C. The left lane

    D. Any lane

    Answer C

18. Always use your seat belt:

    A. Unless the vehicle was built before 1978.

B. Unless you are in a limousine.

C. When the vehicle is equipped with seat belt

Answer C

19. You drive defensively when you:

A. Always put one car length between you and the car ahead.

B. Look only at the car in front of you while driving.

C. Keep your eyes moving to look for possible hazards.

Answer C

20. It is best to keep a space cushion:

A. Only in back of your vehicle

B. Only on the left and right side of your vehicle

C. Only in front of the vehicle

D. On all sides of the vehicle

Answer D

21. Which of the following statements about blind spots is true?

>A. They are eliminated if you have one outside mirror on each side of the vehicle.
>
>B. Large trucks have bigger blind spots than most passenger vehicles.
>
>C. Blind spots can be checked by looking in your rear view mirrors.
>
>Answer B

22. When entering a highway from an entrance ramp, you should generally:

>A. Enter above the speed of traffic to get ahead
>
>B. Enter slowly to avoid other vehicles
>
>C. Stop first, then slowly enter traffic
>
>D. Accelerate to the speed of traffic
>
>Answer D

23. Allowing a space cushion is important because it:

A. Prevents distractions
vehicles

B. Allows you time to
situations

C. Keeps traffic flowing at a safe pace

D. Keeps other drivers alert

Answer B

24. One of the rules of defensive driving is

A. Look straight ahead as you drive.

B. Stay alert and keep your eyes
moving.

C. Expect that other drivers will make
up for your errors.

D. Be confident that you can avoid
danger at the last minute.

Answer B

25. When passing on a multi-lane highway:

A. Be sure the passing lane is clear

B. Pass only on the right

C. Watch for oncoming traffic

D. There is no need to signal

Answer A

26. To make a right turn at the corner, you:

A. May not enter the bicycle lane.

B. Should only merge into the bicycle lane if you stop before turning.

C. Must merge into the bicycle lane before turning.

Answer C

27. Drivers entering a roundabout or traffic circle:

A. Must stop before entering

B. Must yield to drivers in the roundabout or traffic circle

C. Have the right of way if they arrive first

D. Have the right of way if there are two lanes

Answer B

28. Under normal conditions, a safe following distance between your car and the car ahead is:

  A. Fifty feet.

  B. One car length.

  C. Three second behind the vehicle you follow

  D. One hundred feet

  Answer C

29. On two-lane, two-way streets or highways, you should start left turns:

  A. Close to the center line

  B. Close to the outside line

  C. In the center of the lane

  D. Anywhere in the lane

  Answer A

30. teenage drivers are more likely to be involved in a crash when:

      A. They are driving with their pet as a passenger

      B. They are driving with adult passengers

      C. They are driving with teenage passengers

      D. They are driving without any passengers

      Answer C

31. When you are merging onto the freeway, you should be driving:

      A. At or near the same speed as the traffic on the freeway.

      B. 5 to 10 MPH slower than the traffic on the freeway.

      C. The posted speed limit for traffic on the freeway.

      Answer A

32. Collisions can happen more often when:

    A. All vehicles are traveling about the same speed.

    B. One lane of traffic is traveling faster than the other lanes.

    C. One vehicle is traveling faster or slower than the flow of traffic.

    Answer C

33. On long trips you can prevent drowsiness by

    A. Turning on your car radio.

    B. Slowing down so you can react better.

    C. Stopping at regular intervals for a rest.

    D. Moving your eyes from side to side as you drive.

    Answer C

34. To pass a slower-moving vehicle on a two-lane road you must:

    A. Not cross the center line

    B. Flash your lights to oncoming traffic

    C. Use the shoulder

    D. Use that lane that belongs to oncoming traffic

    Answer D

35. When you drive through an area where children are playing, you should expect them:

    A. To know when it is safe to cross

    B. To stop at the curb before crossing the street

    C. To run out in front of you without looking

    D. Not to cross unless they are with an adult

    Answer C

36. When traveling behind a motorcycle:

A. Allow a following distance of at least 2 car lengths

B. Allow at least 2 seconds of following distance

C. Allow at least 4 seconds of following distance

D. Allow a following distance of at least 4 motorcycle lengths

Answer C

37. If you are following a truck that swings left before making a right turn at an intersection, you should remember that it is very dangerous to:

A. Try to squeeze between the truck and curb to make a right turn

B. Apply your brakes until the truck has completed the turn

C. Violate the 4-second following distance rule

D. Honk your horn at the truck driver

Answer A

38. Preparing to smoke and smoking while driving:

A. Do not affect driving abilities

B. Help maintain driver alertness

C. Are distracting activities

D. Are not distracting activities

Answer C

39. The most important thing to remember about speed management and curves is to:

A. Drive at the posted speed limit as you enter the curve, then slow down at the sharpest part of the curve

B. Slow down before you enter the curve

C. Accelerate gently before you enter the curve

D. Drive at the posted speed limit of the roadway, before, throughout, and after the curve

Answer C

40.If you want to get off from a freeway, but
you missed your exit, you should:

A. Go to the next exit, and get off the
freeway there

B. Make a U-turn through the median

C. Pull onto the shoulder and back
your car to the exit

D. Flag down a police officer for an
escort back to your exit

Answer A

41.When no signs, signals, or police tell you
what to do at an intersection, the law states
that:

A. Drivers on the right must yield to
drivers on the left

B. There are no laws stating who must
yield

C. Drivers going straight must yield to
drivers turning left at the intersection

D. Drivers turning left must yield to drivers going straight through the intersection

Answer D

42. Highway hypnosis is a driver condition that can result from:

A. Staring at the roadway for long periods of time

B. Frequent rest stops

C. Too much sleep the night before your trip

D. Short trips on expressways

Answer A

43. To avoid last minute moves, you should be looking down the road to where your vehicle will be in about _____.

A. 5 to 10 seconds

B. 10 to 15 seconds

C. 15 to 20 seconds

Answer B

44. If you stop at a railroad crossing with more than one track:

A. Wait until you have a clear view of all tracks

B. Stop on the railroad track and watch for another train

C. Go through as soon as the train passes

D. Go through when one of the tracks is free

Answer A

45. If you are driving behind a motorcycle, you must:

A. Allow the motorcycle to use a complete lane

B. Drive on the shoulder beside the motorcycle

C. Allow the motorcycle to use only half a lane

D. Pass in the same lane where the motorcycle is driving

Answer A

46. After a train has passed, you should:

> A. Check again for approaching trains and proceed with caution
>
> B. Wait for a green light
>
> C. Proceed across the tracks
>
> D. Blow horn and proceed

Answer A

47. A safe speed to drive your car

> A. Is the posted speed limit.
>
> B. Is less than the posted speed limit.
>
> C. Depends on the weather and road conditions.
>
> D. Depends on the mechanical skill of the driver.

Answer C

48. When driving near a blind pedestrian who is carrying a white cane or using a guide dog, you should:

A. Slow down and be prepared to stop

B. Take the right-of-way

C. Proceed normally

D. Drive away quickly

Answer A

49. Minimum speed signs are designed to

A. Keep traffic flowing smoothly.

B. Show current local road conditions.

C. Test future traffic signal needs.

D. Assure pedestrian safety.

Answer A

50. You are waiting to turn left at a multilane intersection, and opposing traffic is blocking your view, you should:

A. Accelerate rapidly when the first lane you need to cross is clear

B. Wait until you can see all the lanes you need to cross before going ahead with your turn

C. Wait for the opposing driver to wave you across the intersection

D. Edge your car into each lane of opposing traffic as soon as it clears

Answer B

ABOUT THE MASSACHUSETTS STUDY GUIDE

This practical test manual is surely a jinx breaker when it comes to passing your Massachusetts DMV permit license test. Using this practice test guide alongside the Massachusetts driving manual is all you need to ace the DMV permit test. Our over 300 multiple choice questions were prepared right out of the manual to give you the edge as you prepare.

While studying the questions, you will be able to see the correct answer alongside a detailed explanation as to how the answer came about. This would help you not just to know the correct answer, but to understand the reason behind the answer. As you continue to practice with this manual, you become totally knowledgeable and will improve over time. It is advisable you read the Massachusetts driver's license manual before you write the exam. This will enable you get acquainted with all the questions and answers. I hope you enjoy the tests.

This book is split into five categories;

- General Questions

- Road Sign Questions
- Drugs and Alcohol Questions
- Traffic Sign Questions
- Defensive driving Questions.

To achieve a successful test, I would advise you to repeat all the questions till you consistently achieve a minimum score of 85%. Achieving this will help you score much higher when you write the original test.

This practical test has over 300 test question and it is a perfect way to prepare for the actual test. The questions contained here are similar to the actual test questions. Using this practical preparation method as opposed to the time-consuming DMV driver's handbook, you will learn the basic driving skills, road signs, traffic signs, and all about drugs, alcohol and driving. This book will also teach you how to answer the trick questions which always appears on the test.

How to pass the DMV Permit Test on First Try

The learner's permit test can be actually difficult for first-time test takers. It is reported that about 70% fail the test the first time, and probably need to try once again. It is probably frustrating to take the test more than once since you'd have to face the queue again or probably pay another fee which you might not have.

It is now obvious that the best way to pass the test is to pass it the first time and move on without any hassle. It is actually not difficult to pass; you only need to know the secrets of passing the DMV test.

What are the secrets of passing the DMV permit test? I will show you right away;

-   Remember those Small Details

You can engage the DMV manual to know more. It might seem inconsequential and difficult to remember, because they seem less important to driving safety. But you should understand the fact that no knowledge is a waste when it comes to driving and slamming home your DMV permit test.

- **Attend a driver's education class before taking the main permit test**

If the test taker is still in high school, the driver's education class usually ends with the official DMV permit test. The DMV offers some sort of driver's education classes for intending test takers. This learning process is imperative if you intend to pass your permit test at first try.

- **Consult experienced drivers for more explanations**

When you come across experienced drivers who are driving, you can ask questions. This would help you understand the driving process better.

- **Understanding the rules makes it easier to recall**

Most of us might be tempted to cram the road rules questions, but they are quite abstract and difficult to remember. Knowing how to apply it practically might make its remembrance natural for you.

- **Remember to answer all questions**

Any unanswered question is considered a wrong question. It wouldn't hurt making a simple guess on questions you have no clue about. So be sure to fill in answers to all questions.

- **Use common sense and do not overemphasize or think about each question**

- Always answer or solve the easy questions first, and go back to the unanswered or hard questions letter.

- Prepare in advance by practicing and reading all available resources that would help you pass the test.

- Skip any question you have no idea about. Time is crucial when it comes to passing the DMV test.

Made in United States
North Haven, CT
16 December 2023

45927184R00088